The Commitment of the Lark

Poems for Looking Deeply

Pete Armstrong

Spiderwize

The Commitment of the Lark

Poems for Looking Deeply

Spiderwize
3rd Floor
207 Regent Street
London
W1B 3HH

www.spiderwize.com

pjapoetry@gmail.com
www.holybloke.com

ISBN: 978-1-908128-36-2

The Commitment of the Lark

With gratitude to all the teachers who inspire us now, and who have inspired us through the ages.

With particular gratitude to: Mary, Ewan, Robbie and Rowan for being family; Charlotte, Daphne, Steve and Suzy-Anne for dragon's tail on the beach; my wider family for being there; Trevor Blackwell for all the reading and appreciation; Steve Banks for all the mentoring and support; Rolling Tide Sangha for years of inspiration; Gaffers for years of adventures; the CoI for being a community; everyone else for taking me seriously (or not...)

Contents

Preface

These poems were written mostly in the early morning.

They come most immediately from a space of meditation and contemplation.

But behind and around that place are influences that find their way through, especially loving family and friends; compassionate and wise teachers, (particularly Thich Nhat Hanh); deep, inspiring thinkers and clear communicators, (particularly Ken Wilber); and the tradition of English Literature, in which, as a child and young man, I immersed myself.

I want also to appreciate here the shadow: all you difficulties, blockages, blind spots, and enemies, who have challenged me over the years. I could not have got here without you.

These poems have been offered to me, and now I offer them to you.

May we all manifest the commitment of the lark:

> And as I walked down the slopes of Ingleborough
> in the early freshness of an April morning
> the larks rose in front of me, one by one,
> and sang their way upwards against the blue of the sky.

I stood and watched, and listened,
and rose with them, above my terrain,
leading my life in the fullness of wing and beak,
displaying all that I have, the strength of my feathers,
then, song ended, sinking back down to the moor.

If I commit to the path before me I find freedom.
If I back away from the difficulties
I gain the illusory freedom of the fugitive,
skulking, evading capture, leading a lesser life.

The lark launches into air, wind, and song.
May I manifest the commitment of the lark.

A shard of glass gleaming amongst seedling lettuce

A shard of glass gleaming amongst seedling lettuce:
washed clean by the overnight rain,
glinting now in the early morning sun.
I harvest it carefully and store it
on a ledge of the dry-stone wall that edges our vegetable garden.
For twenty-four years I've been collecting fragments,
extracting them from among the broad beans or potatoes,
two or three every session, an indigestible crop.

An irritation surfaces in my meditating mind:
niggling, sharp enough to cut into whatever equanimity I have
and leave emotional energy leaking everywhere.
Even after all these years of practice I'm slow to recognise
this form,
slow to smile my welcome, slow to embrace with
mindfulness and love
this broken bit I buried years ago.
But, if I'm skilful, the irritation, not reburied, held in the open,
may resolve, extraordinarily, into equanimity; glass into onion.

Buried in the past, in the subsoil of our beings,
before rubbish collections, before recycling;
before therapy, before meditation, before love;
churned around for years in the everyday soil of living,
bits of broken sauce bottle, fragments of china cup,
petty humiliations, casual sarcasms,
surfacing now: some sharp, some rubbed smooth,
all so hard, so beautiful, so transformable.

Turning a peculiar blue

I thank you for the bluebell wood you took me to again
We left the footpath
and in the corner of the field
we found the hole in the hedge
and crawled through

I thank you for the shaded space you took me to again
From bright sunlight and green fields
we entered into a place of shadow
hedge beside us, foliage above
tree trunks and bird song close by

I thank you for the dappled light you took me to again
we found ourselves among
the peculiar blue of bluebells
stretching through this patch of wood:
I sat in silence while you stood

I thank you for the bluebell wood you brought me to again
I did nothing
they entered into me
my mind turned a peculiar blue
there was nothing I had to do

I thank you for all you shared on a sunny day in May
We left the bluebell wood
we walked home across the fields;
the bluebells would stay
but now I knew the way

I thank you for this place of love you bring me to each day

Recognising God

If in the silence of the meeting
I open to the presence of God
then who knows how God will show up:
what are my recognition skills like?

I may find hints of God
in the silence and the peace,
but how about in the shuffling and coughing;
how about in the banging of doors
and the entrance of latecomers:
can I recognise God there?

And while I pursue God in the silence,
who is this angry woman who appears
barging into the building,
disturbing our peace,
complaining over the parking:
do I know what sort of cosmic jokes God likes?

And if out of the silence a voice speaks
do I get lost in the words and my thoughts
or might I hear original sound,
shaped in particular ways through a particular being
to create the miracle of mutual meaning:
do I hear voice as God?

And if some words of the heart sutra bubble up
- form is emptiness, and emptiness is form -
to guide me and distract me,
and those thoughts come and then they pass,
like this moment and this meeting:
can I recognise the presence of God in that passing?

No fox cubs playing

Looking down
rolling northern English countryside
on a sunny evening in June
silage fields cut, and silage-to-be waiting
long shadows cast by trees and hedgerows
a pasture with two figures sitting on a grassy slope
no fox cubs playing

Looking out
a shaded copse that may be home to foxes
a bank sweetly peaceful in the summer warmth
wild flowers out now, and flowers-to-be waiting
a new bench, built for Linda who died
small hillocks, secret home to many ants
and no fox cubs playing

Looking within
awareness of breathing, a smile forming
the grass-covered earth pushing up against my body
happiness slowly spreading in me, changing
your presence beside me and within me
the same birdsong entering our hearing
the same fox cubs still not playing

Looking back, looking forward
much is gone, the rest is fading
a glimmering persisting through these words;
we went for fox cubs, stayed for beauty
the realisation that what exists
is the chance to enjoy at any time
the site of no fox cubs playing

For us all

As haunting as the curlew's cry
fluting sound, liquid sound, fading to a dying fall
the loving son, the holy guy
smiling at the scenes spread out before him
gliding serenely through it all

As peaceful as a sultry doze
lying on grass, shaded by ash leaves fluttering in the breeze
the loving son, the holy Moses
leading us all lightly into unknown times
bringing worship to our knees

As graceful as the solid oak
spreading far, growing on, touching heaven far above
the loving son, the holy bloke
writing stories in an inn across the sea,
nudging us onwards towards love

This knowledge of me

Here is a special moment of the summer:
rolling back the cover on the compost heap
laid to rest eight months ago.
Back then this heap comprised dead and dying stuff:
uprooted plants, rotting carrots, cut grass.
Since then the worms have been at work.

Now is revealed dark, rich, compost.
The cauliflower leaves have rotted, tea bags have rotted
the old feather pillow has rotted,
and their ultimate rottenness is this:
pure, fresh, life-feeding compost.

Here is transformational proof,
here is a quiet affirmation of ever-lasting life;
who could doubt the evidence of their eyes?

Revealed in this heap is a meal-in-waiting.
Compost, spread around the broad beans and the onions,
taken down into the soil by worms
sucked up by plant roots as nourishment,
transforms with the sun's warmth into edibility.

Pick and prepare this food,
and eat it in this knowledge of me,
that I am all life,
and that all the universe is within me.

It's a year

It's a year since you died and still you are with me.
As your body faded over the months,
something else grew clearer:
your essence, stripped of its cover,
the steady burn of love at the heart of you.
Seeing it in you, I must recognise it in me;
I am your child and you live within me still.
And I am content now to find it so

It's a year since you died and still you are with me.
The two babies I met yesterday,
were your babies, and you were full of wonder;
their two mothers, devotedly dispensing love,
were your daughters and you were loving them.
In your life you loved indiscriminately.
I am your child and your essence is within me
And I am content now to find it so

It's a year since you died and still you are with me.
At yesterday evening's birthday picnic
your hands brought out food to share
your forethought brought cutlery to use
and your voice invited people to partake.
You sat in the sunshine with us all,
recognising goodness without favour.
I am your child and your love runs through me.
I am content now to find it so.

God in three persons, perfect trinity

God is all, God is nothing;
God is form, God is emptiness,
God is the creator God
God is the disbelief in God
God is perfect understanding.

O my love, be open to me,
let your radiance shine upon me,
and your emptiness fill me,
that my heart may spring open,
and nothing exist between us.
Let us have perfect understanding.

I am the teacher,
we are all teachers now;
I am Jesus,
we are all Jesus now;
I am all, I am nothing;
with perfect understanding
we are all nothing now.

Transformation in the rain

And ah my friends, while the rain teems down,
let us stop here in the woods by the river
and build a fire to sit around.

Let us drop our bags, and scatter to find fuel:
dead branches and twigs still on the trees.
Let us break them off and bring them in, still dripping a little.

And let Simon, with the energy that burns within him,
attend to the lighting of the flame:
apply the spark, catch the tinder, blow the twigs alight.

And while the smoke begins to curl up through the rain,
let some of us assist in building the fire,
and some of us interfere, and we will not know the difference.

Let us drag up a large branch or two, to sit upon,
from where we can comment, and grumble, and joke,
building our damp community in the woods.

And when the flames are warming our thoughts
and turning raindrops into hisses, let Malcolm, oh excellent man,
produce, from his bag, strips of salmon and raw meat.

Let us impale the strips on forked twigs and set them toasting,
some held to the flames, some propped against stones,
and let us watch, through the rain, the transformation occur.

After a period of salivation, let us share out the food we have
cooked:
scorched, blackened, occasionally dipped in ash;
and ah my friends, memorably satisfying.

And when the time has come to resume our journey
let us shoulder our bags and move off in good humour.
May that with which we have been blessed be shared abroad.

Love and devotion

Just a few years after I stopped worshipping God,
I started worshipping you.
I saw only beauty, and felt only welcome.
It was not possible to hold back:
all my best was for you.
In devotion, love made itself.

I followed each stroke of the hairbrush,
and the way you tilted your head to receive it.
I studied the irregularity of your face
and the movement of your bare feet upon the earth.
Your wise insights and mendacity
were equally my book of learning.
Before discrimination, effortlessly,
all of you was perfection.

With the passing years I acquired judgement
and found you wanting.
My character and the tenor of the times combined:
I lost you and much besides.

My journey has been long enough, and hard enough,
for some redemption to occur.
Now I am mostly devoted to practice,
and I practise devotion as I am able.
Sometimes, beyond discrimination,
I softly come home to a place of joy.

May you realise the generosity of your offering
and may I bring gratitude to all that I do.
May we all generate love through devotion,
and may we worship where worship is due.

Wilson Rd, 1976

Skinning up: our regular ritual together.
A certain complex arrangement of cigarette papers
licked and stuck together;
the breaking open of a cigarette or two,
and the placing of the loose tobacco in a line;
the warming of the resin in a lighter flame
and the scattering of the crumbled grains
from between pinched fingers up and down the tobacco;
the rolling of the joint, and final sticking of the paper;
the twisting of the loose end;
the creation of a roach from a piece of torn cigarette packet
and its careful insertion into the other end, the sucking end.

Lighting up: another stage in the ritual.
Application of flame to the twisted paper;
several quick puffs to get the tobacco alight,
a deep drag to fill the lungs, a pause,
and then the exhalation of smoke through mouth and nostrils;
another drag, and then the casual passing on of the joint;
the suckings in, the glowing of the lighted end, the passings on;
smoke and the incense of dope in the room,
voices and incredible string band in the ears.

Going in: the final stage in the ritual.
Breathing is happening, so liquid, so smooth;
sounds are happening, so liquid, so colourful
and shapely in the spaciousness inside;
meaning is flowing from the words, on and on,
the trail of connections is creating silvery lines;
quite large effort is pushing some words out into the room;
there is gutturalness, but across the room a smile is forming:
oh, love gets created in each moment, that's love, that's love;

'dust be diamonds, water be wine,
happy happy happy all the time time time'.

Buddha words

When, in the freshness of the early morning sunshine,
against the backdrop of the garden you love,
the bees, contentedly moving from flower to flower,
are humming harmoniously amongst the red poppies,
consider this: the perfection of the scene
is no more perfect than all scenes, including you.

If, at your work, opening your lunchbox,
you find amongst the lettuce leaves you picked that morning
a poppy petal, blood red amongst the green,
reflect that this gift from the cosmos is no more special
than the gift of all that surrounds you each day.

When, over two or three days, the silky petal
dries to different shades of dark red,
and becomes delicately resilient to your touch,
please extend your enjoyment of the beauty of change
to include the insecurity that you live amongst.

And if, after drought, a thunderstorm comes in the night,
the flashes manifesting through your closed eyelids,
soaking the poppies with rain, consider this:
there is nothing in the universe more deserving of love than you,
and love is saturating you already,
however much your closed eyes refuse to see.

The promise of the depths

Here is not a puddle for a toddler to stamp through,
or frothy rapids for excited adolescents to scream in.
Here is a pool in the bend of the river where we swim together.

We leave our clothes near the grassy bank where the saxifrage
grew,
cross the rocky beach graced recently by cows,
slowly wade in over slippery stones, wait, hip-deep, poised.

The surface of the water is shaded from the afternoon sun by
trees;
unknown rocks and sand on the bottom, unseen fish in the
depths;
the moment comes to lean forward and enter the intensity.

The same silky water that holds you holds me;
our breast strokes make bow waves that mingle as they fade;
your precious body gathers more beauty as you swim.

I cannot touch the swallows as they flit above the pool
nor catch these moments alongside you in the river:
to hold on to you is to sink and drown the two of us.

The river flows from this pool and to the sea.
One day, on the shore, we will hear the silkies calling:
I will take your hand, and we will swim into the depths.

Slow walking meditation

The slowly moving feet in line are walking in the room.
the breathing in, the breathing out, the peacefulness of home.

My feet are placing themselves carefully on the boards,
our path is along the edge of the room to the turn,
along the edge of the room to the turn,
along the edge of the room to the turn.

My eyes are seeing the growing eucalypt through this
window,
my eyes are seeing the eroding hills through this window;
my eyes are seeing the feet behind me reflected in the glass
case.

The slowly walking feet in line are quiet in the room,
the breathing in, the breathing out, the preciousness of home.

We have always been walking in this room
we are walking for ever in this room.

Restlessness is pulling me away.
Returning is knowing right now that here is the only place to
be.

In other rooms, and on the earth, walking is happening;
walking is always happening somewhere,
we are global walking meditation.

The slowly moving feet in line are peaceful in this room.

Beloved brother John walks with me today;
the feet of Buddha, and the feet of Jesus, walk with us today.

The breathing in, the breathing out, the sanctity of home.

Hello little illness

I've got this illness at the moment.
It's making me tired and off-colour:
gives me sweats or makes me cold,
causes me discomfort in my neck.

I'm trying to make friends with it.
A good man recommended this to me.
He said it's good to listen sometimes
to stuff you don't want to hear.

'Hello little illness,' I smile,
'Good to have you along.
I notice you're giving me a hard time:
what's that all about then?'

> *'Ah, got through at last! What a struggle.*
> *You have an unfortunate habit of not listening -*
> *so I have to ramp the volume right up till you do.*
> *Sometimes pain is the only thing that stops you.'*

'Stops me doing what? - I'm listening now, by the way.'

> *'Rushing round in your habitual ways,*
> *damaging yourself and those around you.'*

'Oh. Well tell me more – I'm still listening.'

> *'You noticed yesterday, didn't you,*
> *at the kitchen sink, the pattern of the pain.'*

'I did notice.
I realised that every time I had a thought to do something,
I'd immediately start to do it, almost simultaneously.
But then it would hurt, and I'd have to pause instead.
Turn the tap on; open the drawer; move dirty dishes;
put clean ones away: every little action.
The pain made me realise how often I did this –
sometimes several times every minute, extraordinary.'

> *'Yes, and imagine how many times that adds up to in*
> *a day,*
> *in a week, in a lifetime.*
> *And you also realised what was missing...?'*

'I realised I was doing all these things thoughtlessly,
my mind elsewhere. I was going off on habit.
I was driven by I know not what.
I could see that I do so much without awareness.'

> *'Every time you do something without awareness,*
> *you are probably doing it without love.*
> *When you do something without love,*
> *you risk damaging yourself and others.*
> *Love is too important to leave to chance.'*

> *'Your habitual patterns of doing things were laid*
> *down in the past.*
> *The actions you take now may be loving, or neutral,*
> *or damaging,*
> *but unless you bring your awareness to bear in the*
> *present, you will not know.*
> *You could in small ways be damaging yourself, and*
> *then others.'*

'Well, you know I'm a pretty careful guy.
I don't have any intention of hurting myself or others.'

> *'I see your scepticism – but how do you know you're
> not?*
> *How can you be certain, if you are not conscious?*
> *Yesterday you had evidence – every time you moved
> without awareness it hurt*
> *and you could feel clearly how damaging it was to
> your being'.*

'You're making me think afresh, it's true.
Why don't you tell me what else I should think about?'

> *'Think of it this way: suppose every time*
> *you make one of those seemingly tiny moves without
> thinking,*
> *it's like making a tiny tear in the fabric of your
> being.*
> *You can see, can't you, that hundreds of tiny tears
> every day*
> *add up to some pretty big rents before long.*
> *Think of the energy leaking out, think of your
> integrity lost.'*

'Yes I can see that. I thought I was mostly acting with
awareness,
but this takes it up another level.
Or down to a more detailed level would be more accurate.
I can see there's a lot of work to do…'

'Yes, but do it with joy, love and awareness. Otherwise…'

'… it just becomes more thoughtless, potentially damaging actions.'

'You're getting it. I'm going to go now, and leave you to it.'

'Wait a minute - you're not really my illness are you?
I was thinking you might be my body in disguise, but you're beyond that.
You're the wisdom and the love beyond my sense of self.'

'Perhaps your sense of self has been limited and needs to expand to include me.'

'Sounds a bit scary. What happens if I won't do that?'

'More pain I guess. Sometimes it's the only thing you understand.'

Not another one to love

Across the silent room your face is there,
your being is present.
I have always, over the years, allowed myself
to be fond of you.

Now, some circumstances of the moment
create a small opening:
painfully, reluctantly, my heart creaks a little bigger
as love surges in.

A ripple of energy rebounds through me
bringing tears that I hide.
The words that appear alongside are: 'Ah, so I love you.'
Then: 'Oh no, not another one to love.'

You see, in your life you will experience suffering
and eventually die.
And all of that I will not now be able to ignore
quite so easily as before.

Your joy is now also more of a concern of mine.
In each moment we meet
it's going to be harder now to avoid
giving you my best.

All of this, I know, is to the good. But, I ask myself:
What if it happens again?
What if it happens to other people too?
Where will it all end?

Raspberry topping

You're hanging around at the side of the path
looking luscious and tempting.
You're showing off your ripeness,
the promise of succulent delights.
Millions of years of evolution are strong in me:
I stop, and reach out.

Your juices sweeten my mouth and stain my fingers;
your tiny pips are hard against my teeth and tongue.
I stand and pick and gorge without end.
I am lips and mouth at the end of a tube,
slithering through the world sucking it in.
Your deliciousness transforms me:
I am dark red through and through.

You are the sun and the rain and the earth:
you take them in and, in passing through, they make you.
And now, through you, they are making me.

You are the words of my perfect teachers:
experiences and thoughts passing through purity,
transforming into wisdom and beauty,
offered to the world as love,
available, at any time, as harvest.

Junk and emptiness

A farmer near me harvests junk.
His yard is stacked high with scrap:
old tyres, rusting engines and iron.
There's even an ancient petrol pump.
His tractor can just squeeze between the piles.

Most people think it's an extraordinary mess
but he seems to find it comfortable enough.
He's lived like that for years.

Still, who amongst us
is not in need of purification?

Me, I harvest junk too.
I scour TV and newspapers for second-hand opinions
which I then stash away in my head.
They're piled high in there, slowly deteriorating.

There's not much room to move around
but I'm comfortable with that:
I've lived like that for years.

I know stuff leaks out from time to time
and pollutes my friends and family,
but what's a man to do?

The alternative seems to be emptiness,
and in reality that doesn't bear thinking about.

To boldly go

Last night on our walk in the fields nearby
we came across a hole in the hedge that was not there before.
The hedge at this point is very tall and thick,
and the new hole is therefore like a small tunnel.
We had to go through it of course.

Footprints in the mud indicate we are not the first
to take advantage of the new opening.
Like entering a worm-hole on Star Trek we plunge in.
After a few seconds of gloom we emerge
into the evening light in the field beyond.

This field, sweeping down to the railway,
with the beech grove to one side, is very familiar to us.
To get in we mostly use the stile or the kissing gate.
We have occasionally used one of the four field gates
or climbed the fence on the steep slope by the hay field.

We have entered this field many hundreds of times,
but never at this point: it's like being teleported in.
Just over there is the dead tree with the woodpecker holes.
To be here so effortlessly is like breaking the laws of physics.
A woodpecker flies out of one of the woodpecker holes.

At the bottom of the woodpecker tree we find empty beer bottles,
scattered around by elements of careless local youth.
Another tear in the fabric of the world opens up.
We boldly pick up the bottles and carry them home.
Every moment is a step beyond the final frontier.

The river runs nearby, contributing sound

You all sit round me in silence, feeling my warmth.
Beyond you, the valley sides rise, clothed in trees.
The early morning mist is dissipating into grey cloud.
The river runs nearby, contributing sound.

You all sit round me in silence, feeling my warmth.
Smoke drifts past you, dissolving into the mist.
The fire that burns within me was once trees,
and before that, heat from the heart of the sun.

You all sit round me in silence, feeling my warmth.
Before someone shaped me as a stove
I was a calor gas bottle; before that ore in the ground.
Some of you may find me ugly, and that is a word.

You all sit round me in silence, feeling my warmth.
Tomorrow you will be gone, and I will be cold.
The buzzards will circle in the skies above, mewing.
The river will run nearby, contributing sound.

I once was lost

When I'd been married three months I lost my wedding ring,
which is not a clever thing to do.
I also lost it on my birthday, which was not a great present.
We were staying at a camping barn
with impressive composting toilets up a slope.
I had washed my hands in a cold water basin
and dried them under my armpits.
Probably it came off then.
Several kind people helped to look for it,
but it seemed hopeless,
with all the grass and leaves and mud.

'Don't worry', she said, 'we're still married…'
I knew she was right in the legal sense, but still…
Over the next few days she stopped wearing hers.

I grieved for the empty space on my finger.
I wriggled at the memory of my carelessness.
I didn't realise that cold water would shrink your skin.
No matter how much I tried to re-organise the event in my mind,
the result always came out the same – the ring stayed lost.

When I was nine I lost my father.
They told me he died having a check-up in hospital,
and it's true that he never came home.
But I worked out for myself that they might be wrong,
and secretly kept looking for him.
The searching was hard, and I never found him.

A few days after my birthday, I took courage,
and went back to the scene of the loss.
Alone, in the face of hopelessness,
I concentrated on the tingling of my empty finger,
and my affection for a nondescript band of inert metal.
Starting from the cold water basin,
I methodically scraped back layers of dead leaves,
cut back fronds of bracken, and threw away rotting sticks.

After about fifteen minutes of looking,
in an area I had not planned to search,
just behind a paling fence, and only a few feet
from the large pile of composting shit under the toilets,
I saw a ring lying casually on some dead leaves.

The hardness of the metal convinced me it was real,
and the way it fitted my finger convinced me it was mine.
I sat on the toilet steps while waves of emotion washed
through me.

I had found my wedding ring.
I had found that my father had never left me,
but was always with me in the determination of my actions.
I had found that a world which appears to be
a collection of disparate wrongnesses,
can coalesce into a single world of infinite potential.

The one who is brought within

The one who stands at the door of your church,
whatever its name, seeking entrance,
is transformed by the welcome they receive.
The one who is brought within, and warmed,
and sustained with bread,
can grow into a companion;
you can marvel as their smile arrives,
and at the gifts they bring.
The one who is brought within
is not the same as the one who stands without.
The one who is turned away,
you can never know.

The one who stands at the door of your self,
patient, or angry, seeking entrance,
is transformed by the welcome they receive.
The one who is brought within
is not the same as the one who waits outside.
At first, you may smile to them only,
and that is a start.
Later you may invite them into the hallway,
and begin a conversation.
But when you welcome them fully
and sustain them with love
their true nature can emerge,
not as given,

but instead co-created with you
in the transforming power of that moment.

The one who is turned away,
you can never know.

You are transformed by the welcome you give.

Cupped hands

Under the hanging moon
within the distant thumps of waves
I wander the empty streets of Staithes

The remnant drinkers in the pubs cosy up to the bars
the surfers, satiated on big barrelling waves, dream in their vans
generations of fishermen's wives no longer know every footfall

I stand in the middle of the street outside our house
through the window I glimpse you all so young
laughing in the glow of the fire you all remain so beautiful

Even through the glass your happy animation is palpable
it spills silently out to where I am already half a shade
wandering the empty streets and ways of Staithes

Time is already tipping its way into your hands, cupped or not
it is neither mine to give nor yours to inherit
time is as it is, trickling down, gushing down

As I move from half a shade to full shadehood
may your waves of animation ripple on, ripple on
may you teach your own children well

may they learn to cup their hands
and drink time while they can

With gratitude to all the keiths

I met a seedsman once called Keith.
He was looking round the garden of our community,
a bleak place, high in the hills, and exposed to winds.
We had a conversation I have since forgotten,
but in the middle of it he dropped this inelegant seed:
'If you planted more trees you could create your own micro-
climate.'

It was skilfully done, Keith: quietly, no fuss;
you weren't even looking at me when you did it.
What did 'micro-climate' mean anyway?

The seed sprouted in me and took root;
I read books on shelter belts, I talked, and planned;
I researched grants, and visited tree nurseries.
A little later we planted six hundred small trees.
A lot later they are flourishing larger trees,
with accompanying micro-climate.

Now the other day I met an enthusiast,
a woman full of heart-felt plans to improve the world.
She pushed them at every opportunity, and beyond.

I felt like she was taking a spade to my mind,
and trying to plant full-grown shrubs in there.
Naturally I resisted.

Shrub-lady, you should learn from Keith.

Be a skilful seedsperson:
examine the environment carefully,
select the right things to say at the right time,
drop them in quietly,
move on to the next piece of ground,
have no expectations of recognition or success,
feel satisfaction in the doing.

Thanks, keiths

May you die many times

May you die many times on this day.
May you practice release
from the clutch of the past.
May the old you die,
and give way to the new.

May you emerge from your hole in the ground.
May you brush off the soil
you buried yourself with
and take tentative steps
on the earth.

May you come to the end of the line.
May you come off the rails
you've kept yourself on.
May you wander the land
in delight.

May your weak heart stop beating at last.
May it fail from the stress
of opening to love.
May your new heart
be enormous and strong.

May your rigid fingers be prised
from their grip on the cliff of your life.
May your incipient wings
unfold from your back
and spiral you lightly to earth.

Contemplate the face of love growing old

Perhaps you are fortunate enough to be able to visit your mother,
who has become very old, and whom you love deeply.
As you stand in the doorway of the room,
she looks up to see you, and her face brightens.
Her look is the look of love,
as it always has been.

You know that her memory is fading, as she is fading,
but her eyes still follow you eagerly as you sit down beside her.
Her hand reaches for yours, and presses it.
As she absent-mindedly looks around the room,
she continues to feel your hand and wrist with her thin fingers.
It is the energy of love in her, still glowing.
You feel the warmth of her love being transmitted to you,
as it always has been.

You see how her skin has grown thin, as she has grown thin.
It is patterned with creases, and areas of different colour.
It falls away from her chin in a loose sheet, revealing,
when she moves her head to the side,
the ligaments in her neck.
When she turns to look at you, and you smile at her,
you see her smiling back.
Her skin still moves to recreate the old smile lines on her face.
Her smile has not faded.
It is still an expression of love,
as it always has been.

You see the fading in her hair.
The dark colour has transformed to shades of grey.
It is combed down with a side parting.
The look is familiar to you.
It is the style you have seen in small black and white photographs
from eighty years ago, when she was a little girl.
You are seeing the young girl still present in the old woman.
And in between the young girl and the old woman
is the mother you remember from childhood:
beautiful, fresh, energetic, full of love.
She is fading, but she is still full of love,
as she always has been.

And when the time comes to leave,
and she wants you to stay,
you can dance round the floor a little,
and soothe the pain of separation.
We are still shaped by love
as we always have been.

The Opening, St Andrews 2003

Early on the first morning of my first retreat
Thich Nhat Hanh led several hundred of us,
in silent walking meditation, to the sea.
At first I felt a bit strange,
but then I figured out that what was good enough
for a world-renowned spiritual teacher
was probably OK for me too.

The way led us past silent university buildings
and then, on a public footpath, we crossed a golf course:
the world-renowned Old Course at St Andrews,
the home of golf, where the Open Championship started.
Even this early in the morning there was great busyness
as men worked with machines to cut the grass,
and others waited to tee off by the clubhouse.

Presumably the sight of a long file of people,
led by a diminutive figure in brown robes,
silently and meditatively crossing their hallowed golf course
gave them pause for thought.
Certainly from my new perspective I found
the energy and devotion they invest in their practice
of hitting small white balls into holes with sticks
to be a little odd.

Thay led us to the beach, where he invited a bell,
and we all sat for a while in contemplation.
In this opening moment,
the waves crashed lazily on the shore,
the breeze blew freshly,
and the sand we sat on was gritty.
Later on, we were all late for breakfast.

There is a knocking at my door

There is a knocking at my door.
A determined looking man stands there.
'You have nothing worth saying,' he says.
I try to smile at him, while shrinking a little.
'There may be some truth in that,' I say finally,
'Would you like to come in and talk about it?'

We sit facing each other.
He seems so certain of himself.
'If you do say anything, it will be rubbish.'
'Well,' I say, 'I expect some of my utterings
do come under the heading of clichéd claptrap.
Would you like a cup of tea?'

We sit sipping our tea together.
He seems to come from a different world to me.
'If you do speak,' he says, 'nobody will listen to you.'
'You certainly have strong views,' I say,
and it's a little hard to hear what you say,
'but I appreciate your coming to tell me.'

He gets up to go. 'If they do hear your words,
people will laugh, or be disgusted.'
He seems to speak from bitter experience.
'There's something in what you say,' I reply,
but I guess I have to accept whatever happens.
Sometimes I laugh myself, or feel disgust.'

At the door he pauses.
'You will never come to anything.
Don't even bother trying.
I say this only to protect you from pain.
Do what I say and you will be safe.
There is no-one in the world to trust.'

I reach out gently and try to hug him goodbye.
His body is stiff and unresponsive.
There is hurt held there.
'Thank you for coming', I say,
'I'm grateful for your efforts to look after me,
and I have listened to what you say.'

He heads off down the path.
He seems smaller now, and younger.
I admire his solitary dignity,
and his survival through difficult times.
'Maybe we can work together,' I call,
'See you again tomorrow as usual?'

A map of blunders

It's hard to remember that I have blundered through my life
leaving a wake of destruction spreading out behind me.
Nothing too gross, you understand,
nothing the police would be interested in.

And of course I prefer to dwell on the times
when I have tried to bring more harmony into the world,
and sometimes succeeded.

Still, if I'm going to look back a little,
it's good to be dispassionate about it:
a map is of limited use for navigation
if we simply exclude the features we don't like.

Here's a common experience I'd rather excise:
the innocent friend at school we all took against.
We left special signs about him chalked up on walls;
we enjoyed our cleverness; but he suffered.

There's something a little exhilarating
about the power to create suffering.
On my map, I would have to include too many occasions
where I have taken the special energy of friendship
and tarnished, damaged, or destroyed it.

And I would have to add in also
the continual drip of judgements and irritated thoughts,
translating sometimes into looks or remarks,
influencing others against each other,
spreading out, spreading out:
the contours on the map.

Where is my route through this tangled territory?

to those who have faced me with my errors,
to those who have cut me some slack,
to those who have shown me their suffering,
to those who have forgiven me, and those who have cut me off,
to those who have cleared up after me,
and patched up fractured relationships in my wake,
to those who have responded to my blunderings with
skilfulness:
thank you

to those who have suffered:
I am sorry.

Lessons from Aylesbury

Lesson 1

In my seven-year old mouth, in 1959,
in an old fashioned primary school in Aylesbury,
there is a lump of gristly meat, part of my school dinner,
which I have been chewing forever.

I dare not leave it: leaving food is not allowed.
I cannot keep it in my mouth: the rubbery texture is vile.
I may be forced to swallow it,
but that does not bear thinking about.

In a moment of fearful criminal inspiration,
I surreptitiously transfer it from mouth to pocket.
I have learned my lesson for today:
how to dissemble in order to survive petty coercion.

Lesson 2

Same dining room, different day.
My seven-year-old arms are folded behind my back.
They are twisted peculiarly and they hurt.
All the children have twisted their arms in the same way.

One of the men teachers is punishing us.
He has been very clever in his teaching.
We have learned that we can receive a cruel impulse from another,
and inflict it upon ourselves.

Lesson 3

I am setting off to walk to school.
Autumn is well advanced and it is cold.
My seven-year-old body is shivering,
but I cannot wear a coat.

I joined the school after the start of term
and there was no peg left for me to hang my coat on.
I have learned this: in an environment
of fear and indifference, it may be wisest to suffer silently.

Lesson 4

It is PE time. I am part of a seething mass
of seven-year-old boys hacking at a football in the playground.
There is aggression and shouting and no discipline.
None of us has football boots.

The boys with football boots are on the football field
playing properly, with the teacher refereeing.
To them that hath, privilege shall be given;
to them that hath not, abandonment shall be their fate.

Lesson 5

In the art room the teacher is very happy.
We have produced good work and he has given us stars.
Then someone makes a remark he dislikes;
he turns angry and shouts; he cancels the stars for us all.

As the glowing beauty of my picture fades to mud,
I learn that an arbitrary authority
can transform the happiness of achievement
instantly into bewilderment and silent resentment.

Lesson 6

Over the years I have wrestled with these lessons.
I have toyed of course with anger, and revenge.
By now, the teachers will probably be dead,
so perhaps I should seek out their children, and
grandchildren,
and visit my vengeance upon them,
even unto the fourth or fifth generation.

But instead I have tried to seek out the cruelties within me,
and, using love, transform them into love.
My sweetest revenge is to try to manifest kindness,
and loving consistency, in my dealings with children
(we are all children).
In this I celebrate the survival of my integrity.

I have learned this:
there are lessons we may have the misfortune to learn
that we would do well to decide never to use.

Molar moving on

So farewell then, lower left four, small molar;
drilled, filled and chewed with, over many years;
now cracked, broken and infected,
you have reached the end before the rest of me.

I feel the dentist working at you,
I see the hairs on his wrist.
In the end, you slide out surprisingly easily
from your socket home in my jawbone.

We look at you briefly in the light together.
I see that you are long, slightly smeared with blood.
Then you are gone, and I am left with a gap.
One day the rest of me will go, leaving a slightly larger gap.

In the meantime I do the work required of me,
processing the diet of the world.
We are all teeth in the mouth of life,
moving stuff on, one day getting moved on.

Running aground

Sometimes, while sailing your beautiful boat,
you may run aground, and stick fast in the mud.

If you get angry and blame the mate,
the mate may get angry back and there will be an unpleasant
situation.
Perhaps bad feeling was the reason you ran aground in the
first place.

You need to work together to get the sails down,
so that the wind does not drive you further on to the mud.
Then you can try to push the boat off with poles.
Maybe this will work, maybe not.
Perhaps you will know the feeling of being stuck in the mud
for a long time.

In these circumstances, choices await you.
You can decide to wreck the boat, in anger and recrimination.
You can pretend to stay there, but actually live ashore,
and return occasionally to see what is deteriorating from
your neglect.
You can swap places with some others from boats that are
stuck nearby.

Maybe you climb aboard a boat that is passing by, and sail off.
Usually, round the bend, as the sun sets, another mudbank
awaits you.

As an alternative, you could enjoy the situation you are in.
Maybe there are some advantages to being stuck.
You can study and appreciate your situation.
You can catch up on essential maintenance.
You can have little tea parties with people from the other boats.
You can create love and harmony aboard.

There can be great solidity to life lived on the mud.

One day, if you are alive to the possibilities,
you may notice that some small change in the wind,
together with a quiet alteration in the currents,
is creating an opening.

You can judiciously rock the boat.
If you keep on gently rocking the boat, the grip of the mud
may ease.
You feel the boat slowly slipping off the mud.

Being afloat now requires your attention.

Spiritual triangulation

If George Fox had met Thich Nhat Hanh
I like to think they might have got on well together.
Two radical spiritual teachers,
creating new perspectives on their long-established traditions
encouraging us all to look deeply within.

George, when alive, probably knew little or nothing
about the two thousand year old spiritual traditions,
half way round the globe,
with long histories of experience in contemplative practice.

Today we have access to that knowledge and those skills
in an extraordinary and unparalleled way.
We may find this can be supportive to us
in our enquiry into the nature of reality,
the nature of God,
and the nature of the spiritual life.

Thich Nhat Hanh speaks a lot of God,
and the kingdom of God available to us within, right now.
He says if we are not too attached to the words,
we don't have to choose between different traditions,
we can have double belonging.

Double, or triple, belonging can help us
to see beyond the specific form of practice
and approach closer to the essence of what is.

Think of it as spiritual triangulation,
giving us more precision in our enquiry.

The practices are here, the teachers are here.
Ultimate reality is available.
Where are we?

From still or storm

Waking in the night at South Walsham:
from the silence of the broad
from the stillness of the water
from the cooing of the pigeons
from the yellowness of the crescent moon
from the sharpness of the stars, even unto the little bear
from the spreading glow of eastern red
from the snoring of my crew-mate
and the happiness of my breathing
only one truth comes
we are all this

Waking in the night at Barton Turf:
from the roaring of the wind
from the lashing of the rain
from the dancing of the tree shadows
silhouetted by the boat yard lights
on the inside of the canvas boat cover
from the snubbing of the boat against the mooring ropes
from the yellow gleam of piss in the torchlight
from the snoring of my crew-mate
and the happiness of my breathing
only one truth comes

Armchair rules

Are you sitting comfortably?
Then I'll begin
by saying you need to get rid of your armchair.
It's the most dangerous piece of furniture in your house.
The spiritual health and safety (meditation) executive
has comprehensively banned them,
but unfortunately some do linger on,
posing an appalling threat to your spiritual health.

You know perfectly well that spiritual development
only comes about through the three Ds:
discomfort, distress, and disorientation.

When they appear in your life (and they will)
it's your job to welcome them,
and relish the opportunities they provide
to grow and develop, and to purify yourself.

If you would rather curl up in your armchair,
courting comfort, skulking under a duvet,
you know you are in big trouble.

You know the rules: the more you hide,
the more the big trouble tracks you down
and administers a developmental kicking.

It's better to go out looking for trouble –
then you can meet trouble more on your terms,
and in your time.

So – make friends with a little discomfort,
lean a little into the heat of the fire,
play around the edge of where you're at.
And recycle the armchair.

The freedom in keeping still

The joy of waking up with your child beside you
the joy of keeping quiet so they may continue to sleep
the perfection of their breathing
the perfection of their relaxation
the completeness of their trust in you

Here are a precious few moments
when the night is done
(we are safely through)
and the day is yet to start
(with its unknown difficulties)

Here is liminal space
a freedom, a free time

the sweetness of their breathing
keeps you from drifting
the beauty of their presence
keeps you from wandering into confusion
the depth of their innocence
draws from you the purest love
of which you are capable

drink in the myriad joys of their sleeping
in some moments they will wake
in some further moments they will grow up
and go

follow it all while you can

How to be at home

You are a great gift.
In the dusk I think you are a log lying at the water's edge
but some small movement catches my attention
and we both stop very still staring at each other.

Then you relax and move
and I see your whiskers, and your alert face.
I see wet dark fur on a dog-like creature unfamiliar to me.
You move nonchalantly
turning and investigating in the shallows.
After a while, you take to the water
and swim off in leisurely fashion,
your strange thick tail visible.

I dash forward to the edge of a tiny jetty to see you go,
the ripples spreading out gently from your sleek progress.

Would you let me know
how I can be as at home
in my country as you are in yours?
I have knowledge to trade,
for example on the mind/body question.

You disappear in the dusk, in the water, behind a boat,
and your ripples fade.

Vinegar days

The path winds down through the apple trees
on this breezy August day.
We slowly walk this path, my friends,
in silent contemplation.

Red apples glow, the air is balm,
and the grass we tread is soft.
My hand is held by my sweet friend
and smiles are passers-by.

At a certain moment an old acquaintance comes to join in.
'There's a whole bunch of you,' he points out,
'Walking slowly, holding hands, and not talking.
That's weird. People are looking at you.'

His voice is as tart as the unripe apples.
It shrinks the world and turns it sour.
I turn red inside and try to run away,
but my friend is still holding my hand.

I am ashamedly trapped in this moment,
and all I can do is keep walking with it, burning inside.
Then I remember my manners, and his name.
'Ah, my old friend, acute social embarrassment: welcome.'

'You know', I continue, 'I had always thought that one day you and I would part company and I would never see you again.
It would herald a time of great perfection, and happiness.
Like having sweet ripe apples on the trees every day.'

Ah. A realisation dawns, as impossible perfection fades.
'My friend, I see now that we will always be meeting on the path.
Come and join us, be my companion, hold my hand.
Let us have fun together on the vinegar days ahead.'

A deep appreciation

A deep appreciation
for the wild energy of creation
within and without

A deep appreciation
for the traditions within and without
that wrestle with the energy
and translate it into the Word
and fashion it into the Law

A deep appreciation
for the questing intelligence
that stands on the Word and the Law
and enters the unknown
transforming it into a known -
the elegance of truth agreed

A deep appreciation
for all including and included
in the fundament of our burgeoning
multi-perspectival universe

A deep appreciation
for what goes beyond

We tend not to think it will all be over

The holiday is over.
Packing up to go home is relatively easy:
just stuff everything there is in a few bags,
no decisions to be made.

It may be even easier to go home ultimately:
nothing to stuff in bags,
all the decisions have been made.
The whole shebang is over.

The ballad of the queen of fairies' chair

Across the moor, we follow a dream,
full of the summer joys of love;
in search of the queen of fairies' chair,
as blithe as larks in the sky above

under the sun and beyond somewhere,
we'll sit in the queen of fairies' chair

The moor lies rough, a trackless waste;
we're stepping light and moving slow,
past bogs so deep and bogs so wide,
past the casual caw of a mocking crow

across the breeze and beyond somewhere,
we'll sit in the queen of fairies' chair

With heather and tussocks to stumble upon,
and the rising moor to take us high;
with moss underfoot as soft as down,
the world falls away from the widening sky

above the dale and beyond somewhere,
we'll sit in the queen of fairies' chair

In a lonely place where the curlews call
the chair appears, a chair of stone,
with a seat and a back to rest upon,
old as the hills, old as bone

before tomorrow and beyond somewhere,
we'll sit in the queen of fairies' chair

You sit in front between my thighs
and we both look over the world below;
my arms are held across your breast
as we sit and let the grandeur grow

out of time and beyond somewhere,
we sit in the queen of fairies' chair

Our beings fill up with all below,
outspread as treasure, the world as gold;
we see with eyes through ages past,
we who sit here, lovers of old

out of time and beyond somewhere,
we sat in the queen of fairies' chair

Such devotion to your practice

In the cold pre-dawn dark you rise
and put on your habitual black vestments;
you pad quickly along the empty street,
past the harbour, and along the base of the cliffs.

Leaving behind the vestiges of the everyday
you enter the elemental in an autumn dawn;
congregating in the chosen place,
you sit on your boards together, waiting.

At the edge of the ocean wilderness
you rise and fall with the breathing of the sea;
you are waiting, you are breathing, you are being;
when the wave comes, the moment is all.

When the wave comes, you are up on your board
and dancing at the edge of all that is:
you break open the moment, become the wave,
enter the moment, open the ocean of all.

The wave of the moment is infinite;
if it ends you paddle back to the shrine;
at the ocean's edge you are breathed by the sea
and spat out on to the wave again and again.

As dusk falls into dark you trickle back past the cliffs;
you pad, unattached, through the everyday harbour world;
the sea is empty, the wave awaits its devotees;
another day at the monastery of surf is over.

No network

As a mobile phone, searching for a network
in an area with no reception,
will run its battery down to zero,
so will we also exhaust ourselves
if we spend our time searching elsewhere for happiness.

We may have a friend, a man unhappy with his family
situation.
We may see that he spends his time scanning
all the women he comes across looking for a better mate.
There are many women in the world to check out,
and he will soon find that he becomes exhausted.

We should know that our happiness is not contained
within the body of another person.
Nor beneath the wrappings of the next chocolate bar.
Nor even within the covers of the next wise book on
spirituality.

If our unhappy friend learns to look within himself,
and love what he finds there,
he will discover the source of happiness.
If he cultivates his capacity to generate love,
he can beam out more love;

he can focus love on his unhappy woman,
and he will find that the situation transforms.

Our happiness can only be found in a place
that is not other than
the place of our unhappiness.

We walk, we talk

The landscape of our life together
is criss-crossed with the walks that we have done.
Often we choose a different route,
and open up a new perspective
on the country around our home.
But each time I sing the same refrain:
we walk, we talk, I fall in love again.

Here, from the busy A65, the footpath sign
takes us into solitude and quiet fields;
the traffic fades, and stiles appear;
in warm autumn sunshine we turn on to
an old track, now not much used;
the brambles catch at us, their late fruit is plain;
we walk, we talk, I fall in love again.

Bullocks stand beside the fence, curious;
you enjoy their fluffy coats, and the one with huge ears;
you make friends, but your heart knows their fate;
they do not know, they do not complain;
we walk, we talk, I fall in love again.

By an old stone field barn, the map marks 'well';
we look and do not find it, but I persist;
round the back, sparkling, gurgling quietly,
clear water emerges beneath a wall,
a marvellous sight to nourish and sustain;
we walk, we talk, I fall in love again.

A detour across two fields takes us to a Roman road;
a line on the map, a raised line in the field;
your happiness grows as we approach;
we hop across the straight stream close by,
and discuss Roman soldiers, and Roman surveyors
settling the route through difficult terrain;
we walk, we talk, I fall in love again.

A farm to be bypassed, a muck pile negotiated,
chained dogs noticed, as they notice us;
we cross the main road, and joy for you,
the stone steps you have seen from the car
for twenty-five years are finally trodden;
more paths and little roads take us back to the start;
some memories fade, and some remain;
for me, we walked, we talked, I fell in love again.

Put the camera down, little one

One time I tried to photograph the waves
crashing spectacularly on the rocks,
with blown spray and flung spume,
but the waves laughed at me, and said,

'Put your camera down,
and open your shuttered heart;
let us pound in your veins,
let us rise you and fall you,
and swirl you around in all there is.'

And the wind that was whistling by
laughed as well, and said,
'Point your camera at me, little one,
and see what you can capture digitally.

Take off your clothes instead,
and stand with your arms outspread;
open yourself up to me,
and I will blow clean through you;
there is nothing here that cannot be caressed.'

And the sun and the moon and the stars
that were hanging around smiled, and nodded.
'Let us be your ancestors, little one,
and help you remember,
let your origins be elastic,
let us help you realise all that you are,
and this moment may be forever.'

I am a loathly damsel

I am a loathly damsel and this my fate;
I am assailed by fear and this I do:
cut off that which brings me fear,
and shrink my own domain, in truth,
and shrink my own domain

My mother and father pleased me not:
from them came misery and blame;
and so I chopped them from my life
though I know they still live near, right near,
though I know they still live near

brothers and sisters needs must lapse
they too brought o'er much pain;
and one by one my friends I cropped
in time each did me wrong, sore wrong,
in time each did me wrong

Gawains came by to help, they said,
I gave them all short shrift;
they left confused and leaking fear,
my skill had beat them off, well off,
my skill had beat them off

I keep my hut, I keep alive,
the world out there is crazed;
I'll chop and crop, and crop and chop
till all my fear is gone, far gone,
till all my fear is gone

I am a loathly damsel and this my fate
I am assailed by fear and this I do.

I am confessing this to you now

There is a face that haunts me.
I see it still twenty years on.
Fifteen foot in diameter,
made out of bare branches roughly lashed together,
it leaned against the side of the building
where we were staying, in the woods, by the river.

Its empty eyes saw everything we did
and its lop-sided grin commented sardonically
on the depth of our endeavours.

One evening, in a rush of puritanical zeal,
filled with the determination of righteousness,
that would not be denied,
and the exhilaration that comes from decisive action,
I dragged it from the wall, broke it up,
and burned it on our camp fire.

In my mind I was acting
to protect the precious purity of the place.
The face was wrong, from outside,
left by others, who did not properly appreciate
the spirit of the place.
Simplicity had been sullied, but was now restored.

I slept in peace that night,
but woke very early with a raging guilt.

I saw a group of innocent young people,
happily and enthusiastically working together
to create the face, and leaving it as a gift.
I saw them bringing their parents to see it,
and finding only a blank wall.

There was no way back for me.
The face was ashes, and the ashes were cold.

Guilt burned within me,
and would not be denied.
It drove me to leave my sleeping fellow sinners
(they hadn't stopped me from the burning),
and take to the woods in search of a confessor,
who could take this burden from my being.

That was a wild ride:
the branches and the brambles that caught at me
were blurred in with the turmoil within;
the agony of wrong-doing that cannot be undone;
directionless desperation in the empty woods;
the terror of confession fighting the craving for release.

I found no confessors in the woods.
There was no-one to hear my sins,
and provide the forgiveness I craved.
The tidal wave of guilt that had flung me through the woods
reached its limit, and receded.

I washed up on a steep slope where,
amongst the oaks and the beeches,
I realised that I would always have to live
with the results of my actions.
If I wanted true peace
I would have to learn how to find forgiveness within myself.

Washed out, drifting back,
I found there was, as always,
a new fire to light in the ashes of the old,
and a new day to negotiate.

Faint shadows of flowers

In the silence of the dawn, I wake up from my dreaming mind;
the candlelight throws faint shadows of flowers on the wall.

Ah, my dreaming mind, you have been a friend to me,
been with me through difficult times:
you were always there with fantasies of better futures,
and a comforting reshaping of a troublesome past;
thank you for your lifetime work.

In the silence of the dawn, I wake up from my dreaming mind;
the candlelight throws faint shadows of flowers on the wall.

As a child, to discover you was an amazing joy:
a secret world within, not available even to my mother,
a better world, full of endless delights;
as a child, even with love, the way is hard;
the world rolls on, and we are so small.

In the silence of the dawn, I wake up from my dreaming mind;
the candlelight throws faint shadows of flowers on the wall.

To know you is to feel a surge of affection for you:
like old friends, we know what we have survived together;
like true friends, we know now our ways are parting:
we will meet up occasionally, and reminisce with love;
thank you for your help through troubled times.

In the stillness of the dawn, I wake up from my dreaming mind;
on the wall just in front of me, faint shadows move delicately:
the candle on the windowsill is silhouetting the vase of flowers;
through the window, trees and lawns are appearing:
my knees ache slightly, and we are about to stand up.

'I am blooming as a flower'

I admire the tenacity and complexity of ivy.
If you look closely at ivy on a garden wall,
you will see that over many years
it has penetrated the cracks between the stones,
expanded over a wide area,
clung everywhere to the rough surfaces,
grown back on itself, interpenetrated itself,
died back in places and then grown again on top.

It has created a dense, tangled, clinging mass.
It reminds me a lot of my own mind, which I also admire.

Of course we prefer to think of our minds
as sophisticated instruments of intellectual clarity,
and there is no doubt some truth in that.

If a spiritual teacher then tells us that happiness is very
simple,
and that we can realise it by becoming as fresh as a flower,
the ivy part of us naturally becomes a little upset:
'I've spent years developing my dense complexity attached
to this wall.
I am sophisticated and urbane.
Happiness will one day emerge from my ever-increasing
sophistication.'

We can perhaps reassure ourselves at this point.
There is no requirement to abandon our precious intellect
(though some judicious pruning might not go amiss).
Ivy has a beauty of its own, and a place in any garden.

We can however, in contemplation and appreciation,
track back into the depths of our minds,
trace where the trunk thickens closer to the ground,
notice the flow of energy emerging from the roots,
and follow these back deep into the soil of our being.
There the seeds of many flowers await,
ready to germinate and grow.
In our garden, there is infinite space
for the simplicity of happiness to bloom.

Riddle me this

Moses found me in the fruit of the bush that burns
but you could go to the high place in Edom
and eat of the thorn apple, and sweat, and be on fire
and I may not speak to you.

Shamans found me in the dark of the caves
but you could go to the Dordogne
drum and chant for days
sit at the end of the deepest tunnels
and I may not appear to you out of the rock.

George Fox found me at the top of Pendle Hill
but you could climb a steep hill in Lancashire
and stare out over the land
and I may not visit you with a vision
of a people to be gathered.

You don't have to travel to find me
but you do have to find your own way.

I am not outside you, and nor yet within you
but if you inhabit these two areas together
so they are not-two
you will bring me near.

I am always between yesterday and tomorrow.

Sometimes it's very hard

There are some hard tasks in life.
I know a woman whose husband has died.

On New Year's morning she has to go
into her young sons' bedroom, and tell them.
That's hard.

Fresh from the rawness of the news
she is grieving so much herself;
now she has to look at her beautiful children,
innocent and unknowing,
and prepare to tell them something
she knows will break their hearts.
That's hard.

She has to change their lives forever;
it has to be done;
all sorts of things have to be done now;
there's no escape.
That's hard.

Then she has to comfort them
while they cry into their breakfast,
while her own heart is hurting.

And she is alone now,
no man to help her with the hard tasks.
He's dead now, you see.

Into the wind

To learn to sail from a book would be hard.
It's easier to watch other people,
get their guidance, and benefit from their experience.
At some point though,
we still have to steer the boat ourselves, and do it.
We may learn to make progress through the water.

Learning meditation from a book is also hard,
though sometimes needs must.
Even with loving help and guidance though,
there comes a time
when we have to sit on the cushion ourselves, and do it.
We may learn to realise more deeply what is.

Unknown sailors over many generations
have developed clever arrangements
of masts and sails, of tiller and keel.
Skilful use of these enables us to sail in any direction.
We can even use the power of the wind to sail into the wind.
Not directly – the progress we make is in the form of a zigag,
but the thrill of tacking into the wind
brings a liveliness to the boat, and to us.

Known and unknown teachers over many generations
have developed clever ways and means
to help us develop greater awareness.
If we use them skilfully we can overcome our inertia and get
moving.
We can use the practices to keep us moving,
despite the contrary forces in us and around us.

Eventually we may learn how to face into any difficulty,
any resistance or barrier, any doubt or distraction,
release the energy trapped in there,
and utilise the power of the difficulties to move us through
the difficulties;
we make progress on our journey.

This may require a lot of our attention and concentration
– these are sometimes powerful forces -
but we may find, as we get more used to the bumpiness of the ride,
with the boat leaned over and the water foaming at the stem,
that this becomes our favourite point of sail.

Your heart's desire

As though in a dream, wandering the land,
I come across a shrine, and enter in.
An old man sits silently and smiles.

A question bubbles up within me
and floats into the space between us:
'How can I be happy?'

I hear only kindness in his voice:
'Wait a little in this place, and consider:
What is your heart's desire?'

In the pause, I know the answer
is not about more holidays.

And then into the silence,
a voice begins to sing sweetly
bringing happiness to the room;
it is my heart, answering for herself:

'I wish to give love, on and on,
more and more, without stint.

I wish to be wide open to the joy
of this immeasurable life.

I wish to be with God again,
beyond words, as love.'

The old man fades, as does his smile,
the room too disappears, as though in a dream.

The echo of the song remains.

The one who sits in a room

The one who sits in a room and speaks with love
dissolves the boundaries between us;
the greater the love, the greater the dissolution.

The one who sits in a room and speaks with love
speaks not to us, but to themselves,
because they know they are not other than us,
and we are not other than them.

The one who sits in a room and speaks with love
creates a loving presence that fills the room,
and bathes us all in a love
that finds ways through any cracks in our rigidity,
and makes it harder for us to hold ourselves aloof from love.

The one who sits in a room and speaks with love
has grown larger than us and can contain us within them;
they open their being to us, and if we enter in
we will find ourselves on the inside of love,
and from the inside of love, all is revealed.

And what happened to you, little boy?

And what happened to you, little boy?
The last time that I saw you,
you were kicking your legs out with joy,
in the stackyard, while the geese ran past,
and the adults worked the farm around you.

Oh the usual bewildering mix
of joy and sorrow
left its mark upon me;
I tried to claim exemption from the pain,
but I failed.

I sat in the kitchen by the fire,
felt the warmth, watched the flames,
and ate the food cooked upon it;
my job each morning was to rake out the old,
and set the new to burn.
I tried to claim exemption from the ashes,
but I failed.

I heard the adults singing in the day,
a bubbling trail of laughter and of joy;
but as I learned those songs,
I began to hear beneath,
some crying and some wailing in disguise.
I tried to claim exemption from the choir,
but I failed.

Bewilderment stayed close
while the geese and adults left,
and I grew too old to march alone in joy;
for some reason I stayed on,
living more and more what's here.
I'd tried to claim exemption from my life,
but I'd failed.

I will wait for you in the dark

And I will go with you into the caves
into the darkness, under the earth
leaving this world for another
by the flickering light of torches

We will encounter petrified columns
slow-formed through many lifetimes
and sinuous curves and smoothed walls
shaped by water flows, in untold passages

At the place of the red ochre
I will anoint your skin with the earth
and your flesh will gleam white and red
by the flickering light of torches

We will drop deeper into the earth
through cracks and fissures in the rock
find new caverns in the dark
and hear the distant sound of water falling

And if you need to go beyond alone
I will wait for you in the dark and sing
and when you return I will welcome your ochred body
by the flickering light of torches

The emptiest field in the world

On a path by the river,
in a lonely valley with trees and birdsong,
having left behind our home,
we come to a gate.

We stand at the gate and pause;
beyond lies the emptiest field in the world;
we know it for the unknown;
our eyes, ungirdled by routine or expectation,
see it clearly: startlingly empty, deeply unknown.

One of us takes courage and opens the gate,
deliberately goes through and strides into the field,
confidently, with awareness,
right into the middle and beyond,
an act of bravery.

One by one in silence we others
loose our hold on the familiar,
pass through the gateway,
take steps into the empty field,
take steps into the empty field.

The school gate is near enough, thank you

At first you are glad when your mother holds your hand
and takes you into the classroom at school;
later on, the school gate is near enough, thank you;
at eighteen you prefer her not to sit in lectures with you,
no matter how much she would like to look after you there.

When you first move into the realms of intimacy with
another,
your lively and familiar friends miss your presence,
but it would not work to invite them along:
their sense of humour would get in the way.
Sometimes it is necessary to shut the door on friends.

If you are ready to realise a larger freedom,
and a deeper connection with all that is,
you will find your thinking mind does not easily accept
the existence of a reality beyond itself;
but you have to leave your thinking behind for a time,
if you wish to practise the art of meditation.

A welcoming mother at the end of a hard day,
your friends' jokes as a respite from intensity,
a rational review of what was realised:
on your return, all of these are worth appreciating,
not abandoning, however far you have been beyond.

Rules of engagement

When you snipe at me
I will not disappear.
I will dodge your projectiles
make clever use of ground cover
and approach close enough
to disarm you

When you strike at me
I will not run away, or strike back.
I will skilfully deflect your blows
with my shield of love
and approach close enough
to disarm you

When you retreat into armed neutrality
I will not so retreat, with relief.
I will wave my banner of love
and approach close enough
to instigate a summit of joy

I will search within me
for any reasons
to treat with you in ways
that are less than love
and reject them

This is my holy quest
in which I will persevere
through difficult times

A melodious burst of water drops

A melodious burst of water drops
hits the surface of the water next to me,
wakening me to my surroundings.

In stillness, I am on a narrow strip of land
surrounded by a profusion of tall trees
between a mere and a gently curving canal.

Looking up, I see high above me
a squirrel leap gracefully
from one slight branch to another.

The branch sways, drops of water
are dislodged from twig and leaf;
they fall down and down through the air.

A melodious burst of water drops
hits the surface of the water next to me,
reaching my ears, evoking joy.

On the water, in the air,
the ripples spread and spread,
mixing into the reality of this world.

No favourites

Like the loving mother who has no favourites
amongst her large and lively family,
we can sit at the noisy kitchen table with our brood
and dispense love and attention where needed:

to the one who works hard, and the one who dreams,
the one who gets angry, and the one who smiles,
the one who rushes, and the one who dawdles
the one who looks after our body, and the one who is
careless;

when we know they are part of ourselves
it is not possible to neglect any of them;
if we do neglect them,
we know the one who neglects
particularly requires love.

Pain

When pain afflicts you, it can be difficult to think.
However, if you are able to, you may care to reflect
upon the following:

If you are feeling pain, it is proof you are alive;
you may like to be grateful for this.

You are descended from a long line of pain-bearers;
most of your ancestors lived out their lives
without paracetamol, anaesthetic, or GPs;
those who couldn't bear pain probably died out;
think of them all with gratitude occasionally.

Your body works assiduously to preserve itself;
over millions of years it has become very clever;
it has worked out that pain is functional.

Ask who the pain-maker is in you;
consider treating them as a friend rather than an enemy;
it is likely they are doing their best for you.

Please remember to appreciate all your pain–free days,
when they happen to come along.

Be properly grateful for modern medicine.

Just as we should correctly see
the whole winter flood plain as the bed of the river,
not just the summer winding course,
so we may like to appreciate our life
as comprising the full range of experience
not just the pain-free parts.

Please note that reflections upon the nature of pain may,
or more likely may not,
lead to actual pain-relief:
that, on the whole, is a different matter.

Adding another dimension

It seemed to be the pine that opened my eyes and more.

I was looking down over Leighton Hall and Leighton Moss
with Morecambe Bay and Arnside Knott beyond,
and the Lakeland fells in the distance:
a view of beauty and delight.

Some little shift occurred within me,
and I saw the pine stand out from its smaller fellows,
and realised it stood in space.

Scales fell away from my eyes:
the scales of window panes and windscreens,
flat-screen TVs and photographs,
Turners and Constables,
and the tops of chocolate boxes.

The pine was in the world,
and I could walk around it.
The world was all around me,
and I could wander in it.

I walked back down the lane,
and practised my revelation.
The trees remained in 3D,
emerging surreally from the earth.

I walked backwards for a while;
the world was still real behind me,
and I was still moving in it,
a joyous pilgrim of the pines.

Snared by tradition

We found the old snares in the barn,
thin nooses of twisted wire
that slid easily through a loop at the end.

We were boys excited by the possibilities of action,
and the long tradition of the hunt;
we set the snares in gaps in the hedges around.

Early next morning, from the bedroom window,
we could see two grey shapes
lying at the far edge of the next field.

The excitement of the catch took us there:
the two hares had likely been chasing each other
through the fields and hedges, courting.

The scrabbled earth around, and bits of fur,
indicated their strangulated end had been slow;
the deep embrace of the noose was our aim, not theirs.

Released from the wire snares, we carried them back;
held by the back legs, the bodies were a dead weight,
and the heads swung loosely, with bloodied necks.

Aaron Hart the butcher came to look at some beasts
and we sold the hares to him for half a crown;
somebody somewhere ate them, maybe jugged.

We checked the snares regularly after that
but always found them empty;
we were boys, growing up in the tradition of the hunt.

A mind of its own

I thought I was in charge of my own mind,
but this turned out not to be the case.
I thought I would change my mind,
but it turned out my mind decided
when it would change me.
My mind had a mind of its own.

Whenever I looked,
there was a whole lot of stuff going on in there
that seemed to have little to do with me.
What was this 'me' anyway?
I was becoming more doubtful than ever.

I thought I knew my own mind,
but this turned out not to be the case;
when I began to probe,
there didn't seem as much there as I thought:
nothing solid,
just a cloud of thoughts
forming and reforming continuously.

As it all looked quite comforting
I thought I'd lie down in the cotton-wool
and fall asleep.
Maybe I'll wake up again some time.

There is nothing about you that I do not love

There is nothing about you that I do not love.
And in being with you I have learned
that there is nothing about myself
that I cannot love.

In your presence my shame fades,
all the sorrows of my life have meaning
and a current of love animates my smile.

I could strip myself to the bone before you,
open the locked doors of my being
and let the unsavoury innards spill out,
and there would be nothing
you have not already seen,
and understood, and loved.

You make no effort to hold on to me.
Leaving you is easy; and I forget you frequently,
but when I return, in a heartbeat,
I am basking in the glow of your presence
as though I had never been away.

The smile of your greeting
is never other than love;
the depth of your being
is never less than infinite.
There is nothing about you that I do not love.

Homeward bound

I was twenty-one years when I nearly wrote this poem.
I'm fifty-eight now but I won't be for long...
ready or not, life hurries on,
and my youth, that was green, turned to brown.

Hanging out in a garret, misunderstood,
I was a rock, I was an island.
Other people bowed and prayed
to the neon gods they made,
but I turned to Simon and Garfunkel
and, with my headphones on,
I took some comfort there.

The darkness was my old friend
but I still longed for someone with whom
I could harmonise till dawn.
Eventually I found April, come she will,
to break my heart,
and shake my confidence daily.
I was afraid to get up to wash my face
in case I found, when I got back to bed,
someone had taken my place.

In the wasteland of my youth,
I turned to the wisdom of a poet and a one-man band,
and I still carry the reminders of every song
that cut through my sound of silence.
The poems I mean to write
still fade in the night.
And many of my words come back to me
in shades of mediocrity.
But, like emptiness in harmony,
it's good to be homeward bound.

The deep upwellings of the night

In the deep upwellings of the night
you ooze into me.
My struggles against you are in vain
and I retain only the aches and pains of resistance.
My defences pop like tacks out of the floorboards
as the lino rises to the pressure
of the flooding tide from the cellar.

You ruin my old ways,
they no longer function or serve,
and I must cast them out.
Your creeping power overcomes all my clinging,
unless I am willing to drown.

May I float free and learn to survive;
may I rise with you,
and welcome the dawn
illuminating the new world we are creating.

The first home of your own

Do you remember yours?
Mine was in Bardwell Road,
a top flat in a big house,
entered through a thick curtain
with a bell on it.

The space inside was perfect,
because it was ours.
The kitchen had a shelf outside the window
instead of a fridge,
a wooden draining board that smelled bad,
and a gas cooker from the ark.
We rejoiced in it all.

In winter it was unbelievably cold.
I tried to heat my room with a paraffin stove
called Humphrey.
I learned to warm my hands
round my mug of tea in the morning.

A small group of us created our home here:
an extraordinary swirl of affection,
words and attitudes, constantly refined.

We filled the space with exotica:
a stream of friends and other guests,
bringing themselves and their strangeness
to be imbibed and digested.
An engineer called Annabel
made us a kedgeree.

Mrs Nimmo-Smith sat in her kitchen
on the ground floor, with cats and dogs,
and received our monthly rent cheque.

In the end it all came to an end.
We finished it with Titanic,
a going down party.

The praises of older women

in the dark cold of midwinter
we will walk through the snow
and gather with our families
in the building that our ancestors made
and we will sing praises
and we will sing praises

tonight we will stand before you
with hair from grey to white
in the place we remember from girlhood;
we will look at you as you look at us
and we will sing praises
and we will sing praises

in this building soaked with praise
you may close your eyes on our age
and hear the loveliness of young women:
our voices have not grown old
for we have sung praises
for we have sung praises

and if love starts to move in you
your love will inform our praise
which rises up beyond this place
and spreads out all around
and then settles gently down
and then settles gently down

As, on a starry Christmas night

As, on a starry Christmas night,
with the sharp cold pinching at your nose,
and the frosty snow crunching underfoot,
you may co-operate with your family
to set fire to a waxy card
at the base of a large paper lantern,
and watch the envelope slowly fill with hot air
so that the lantern starts to take on a little life of its own,
tugging and moving gently in your hands...

As, on a starry Christmas night,
when the moment is irresistibly right,
you may release the lantern
so that it soars straight up into the night-time,
shooting up towards the stars,
translucent white light and orange fire dwindling,
stretching your being as you rise with it,
so that your flimsy fragility
rejoices in the endless dark liberation
opening around you...

As, on a starry Christmas night,
with the moon rising large in the east,
and the voices you love exclaiming round you,
and the crunch of frosted snow below,
you may glimpse the beauty of our beginnings,
and the outrageous courage of our journey
into the unforeseen
and the spark which illuminates momentarily
the illusion of solidity in our lives...

...so may we all encounter joy

Today we started to plant a wood

It's not every day you set out to plant a wood.
In that dead time between Christmas and New Year
we set off down the field with tubes and stakes
and a bag containing twenty-five young oaks.

The ground was still frozen in places;
some mist hung around in the valley
and we saw the river below was running high,
melt-water sweeping past left-over ice on the banks.

We discovered it's not so difficult to plant a tree:
with your spade you cut the turf and dig a hole,
put the little tree in, replace the soil nicely round the roots,
and tread the soil down carefully.

It's good to add joy and laughter and love,
but the tree will probably grow anyway, given sun and rain;
It's good to reflect on beginnings, and courage, and faith,
but the translucent protective tube may be more important.

If you repeat all this twenty-five times in a morning,
the ghost of a wood emerges on the land:
it was probably over a thousand years ago
that there was last a wood here.

We trundled our spades and lump hammer back home,
and ate heartily of baked beans for dinner.
Tomorrow, there are many more trees to get in the ground,
but today, today, we started to plant a wood.

The life of fear and anxiety

I particularly like to join people at their meals;
they are often pretty relaxed then, chattering away;
of course as an uninvited visitor I'm not welcome,
but I have got used to that, though it still hurts a bit.

The convention is that everyone pretends I'm not there;
they wipe my presence from the table, then wipe the wiping.
I'm left feeling pretty ignored, and empty;
I have to say the life of invisibility is not fulfilling.

So while they are nattering on, or watching TV,
I just slip on down with the food.
If they paid proper attention I couldn't do it,
but hey, I didn't ask to be made into a ghost.

Once down there I like to make myself at home;
later on they complain of cramps, and indigestion;
they say its bloating, and stop eating wheat.
Suits me, I have to hang out somewhere for a while.

The weird thing is I don't actually need much:
just a small place on the team, a bit of attention,
the chance to protect and advise,
a warm basket by the fire, so to speak.

So think about it – and here's a motto for you:
let your teeth chatter a bit more,
and your tongue a bit less.

A real musician

I was in a band once.
We mostly just liked playing for ourselves,
and sometimes for a few friends,
but one time we actually got a gig, at a party.

We were pretty nervous setting up in the hall,
but we tuned our instruments,
and did our sound checks,
and then went off to sit in a car round the corner
for a slightly paranoid smoke.

We were part way through our precious songs,
to, as far as I could judge,
polite indifference from the few people
chatting at the far end of the room,
when a man appeared
and started to set up his keyboard beside us.
He then began to play along.

We looked at each other in puzzlement.
We knew him vaguely as a real musician,
but did he not realise this was our first gig?
Not being Oasis and not wanting to make a fuss,
we had a quiet word.

He was keen to join in,
and we were embroiled at the time in idiot inclusivity,
so we let him.
We told him our songs were special,
we'd rehearsed them a lot,
and he needed to play with sensitivity
in order not to ruin them.

The musician added his crashing chords
and ruined the songs.
The people at the far end maintained their indifference.
We gradually understood who the real musicians were.
And as for our gig:
we'd taken the Oasis test, and failed.

Waiting for the great spring

Sometime in the late autumn
a visitor took up residence in my little room.
Next to my portrait of a stern Zen master,
a butterfly had folded its dark wings back,
attached itself to the wall and, unmoving, just stayed there.

I wondered if it were dead and slowly dessicating.
That's how I sometimes feel myself.

On New Year's Day, in the morning,
the forty-ninth anniversary of when I heard my dad had died,
my butterfly woke up;
I had made the room very warm
while I was half-naked, cutting my hair.

The butterfly fluttered against the window, trying to get out.
I resisted the simple urge to open the window
and let it out into liberation and death.
Instead I carefully drew the blind,
turned down the heating, and left.

When I returned a little later,
the butterfly was asleep again in its old position
next to the Zen master.
I was very happy.

Now when I look at the two of them together, I smile.
I know that all three of us are alive,
a small family sharing this little space,
until the great spring returns.

A moment of pattern and novelty

Yesterday I was a man who knew everything;
today I am a man who knows nothing.

Yesterday I sat in the coffee house among friends;
today I am in the alien territory I thought I wanted.

I have only vague knowledge from a theoretical map,
a distant perspective on familiar landmarks left well behind,
and the faith that, in the past, I have gone into
other new territory, and come out alive.

Uninhabited territory has no people in it.
The dawn comes up on greyness I do not know.

I know that even if one day I return, there is no going back.
That which was familiar with friends will have shrunk,
that which I cannot communicate will have grown.

Each moment has pattern and novelty;
I have entered newness of my own volition,
but my volition has novelty patterned into it;
there is no option to not go on.

No thanks Galileo

Galileo:
'Here's my new instrument, a telescope.
Look for yourself:
the moons go round Jupiter
as the earth goes round the sun.'

Inquisition:
'No thanks.'

Post-rationalist:
'Here's meditation, inner contemplation,
and an extraordinary new mix now available
of eastern tradition and western psychological insight;
if you apply yourself to it
in a disciplined way for some time
the clarity of your perspectives will increase
and that which is hidden behind all,
that some call emptiness,
and some call God,
and some call Buddha nature
may be glimpsed.
Try it for yourself.'

Rationalist:
'No thanks.'

Bent and swaying on the path

If, like me, you suffer from vertigo, you will understand
that the time I found myself part way up
a precipitous cliff path in Devon
was not a happy one.

The haven of the cove, with its attractive beach,
was a long, long way below;
the security of the rolling land at the top,
with its absence of death drops, was way above.

I was in the middle, finding it increasingly hard to move,
as powerful images of my imminent fall
through empty space
crowded in on my jagged and petrified mind.

Under the pressures of the ordeal
my being bent and swayed on the path;
I looked to bale out from reality, but I had no parachute
to float me down to the warm sands below.

Instead a question rose up to save me,
perhaps emerging from the solid path
on which I stood so shakily:
am I falling at this moment?

The realisation that I was not falling in that moment
enabled me to take a non-falling step;
in the next moment, it turned out, I was not falling either;
a succession of non-falling moments took me to the top.

From there I saw the sun shine on the waves
creating sparkling momentary light in the world;
I saw, while gulls soared on the warm air,
that at the heart of each moment, fear is not possible.

How to hold back, how to let go

One time, at the farm, we had a craze for building dams;
at the farthest point of the bottom pastures,
in a little valley, shaded amongst a few trees,
we chose the perfect spot, away from adult eyes.

The beck here chattered shallowly over stones,
the far bank sloping up high to the skyline;
the near bank was low, but steep and overhanging,
perfect for making the turfs we needed.

We worked so hard, stamping at the edge of the bank,
making the indents of our heels deeper and deeper,
till the piece of turf dislodged, soil attached beneath,
and we humped it over to the line of the dam.

We built it up slowly, turf on stone, turf on turf;
cleverly we left a gap in the middle for the beck to flow
through,
to give us time to build up the rest high enough;
a long time we spent, in boy time, but satisfying.

When all was ready we collected a final load of turfs,
then quickly, excitedly, heroically, we filled the gap;
we had dammed the beck, we had stopped the flow;
downstream started to empty, upstream to fill up.

Filling up was slow, and, hungry, we went back for dinner
spiced by the secret knowledge of the changes on the beck;
rushing back down afterwards, we found a lengthening pool
edging its way to the top of the dam, the great moment near.

The letting go, ah, the letting go:
the jumping down into the empty stream bed,
the dislodging of a few turfs in the middle,
the start of flow,
the leaping out on to the bank,
the flow increasing,
the weight of water suddenly rushing,
gouging instantly a gaping gap,
the surge, the final flood,
the wall of brown water,
racing down stream,
small boys running alongside on the bank
trying to catch every detail,
before it all dissipated.

And afterwards, returning slowly to the dam,
we surveyed what was left, began again,
collecting scattered turfs from the stream bed.

We had a craze for building dams, and letting go.

The greater wisdom

When I try to speak wise words
and share my understanding of the moment,
you tell me what you are aware of right now,
in all the shifting beauty of this moment,
and I bow to the one who is manifesting the greater wisdom.

We fathers

we fathers take our sons to the beach
on a winter's morning in the dark
and leave them heading into the crashing waves
to ride the surf of excitement all day long

we fathers teach our sons to drive
and watch them set off on the metalled roads
to take their chances amongst the crashing cars
with the thrill of life rushing through their veins

we fathers take our sons to the edge of the city
and see them disappear into the hive of streets
to try to survive and make their fortunes
amongst the crashing hopes and dreams

we return to the beach at nightfall and wave our torch
dark figures detach from the sea and come home with us
mostly our sons return OK, mostly our sons return OK
mostly our sons return OK

My favoured reality

a drear day dawning through the window,
grey silent mist closing in,
leafless black trees, yellowed grass in the field

inside the house a joyless silence
resounds with last night's miserable
miscommunication and misunderstanding

further inside, a melancholy mind
contemplates life's failures so far
and shrinks from the ones to come

in some alternative universe
somebody is longing to experience
the good fortune of this triple whammy

they are lamenting another day to endure
of relentless sunshine, boring harmony,
and troublesome joie de vivre

the wall between these realms is satisfyingly solid
built up in mind over generations –
a quick glance, and then back to my favoured reality.

Holding on, letting go

Sometimes my dad lifts me on to his shoulders
and I ride along, sitting up there.
He holds on to my feet, and I hold on to the top of his head,
and I get a good view of everything.

One time he was talking to my mum about stuff –
attachment, and the importance of letting go,
and freedom from views and other boring things,
but they seemed to really like it all.

He got so carried away he started to wave his arms around.
When I saw them waving in front of me,
I knew they couldn't be doing their proper job,
which was holding on to me, and keeping me safe.

He'd let go all right – he'd let go of me.
For some reason this made me hold on much tighter:
I grabbed his hair with one hand,
wrapped my other arm round his face at eye level,
and tightened my legs round his throat.
That brought him back to the present moment.

He stopped walking, and he couldn't really talk.
He got hold of my legs again and I relaxed a little bit.
My mum came and lifted me down to the ground.
I saw her give my dad a hard stare.

We finished our outing with me walking between them,
holding them both by the hand. I like that.

The offering

I heard this question one time in the island grove
where we were gathered in the early morning:
'How does a perfect teaching work?'

An offering dropped gently into my being
as though into the clarity of water;
it was itself as transparent as water
so that its slow progress down was visible
only as the slightest ripple in the stillness.

At a certain depth
the offering transformed in a moment
into shimmering blues and greens and reds,
a kaleidoscope of bubbles and colour,
spreading out,
bringing the beauty of the rainbow to my being,
softly exquisite and benign,
lingering on and on and on.

Mist

In the early dawn of this autumn morning,
the mist congregates on the leaves of the large beech
tree,
and drips, leaf by leaf, to the ground.

In the silence of the orchard,
the apples hang dark red on the branch,
waiting in the mist, moistened by the mist.

In the wet grass the men practise their martial arts:
their sticks clash rhythmically,
their deep shouts penetrate the mist.

In the silence of the rising sun,
the sunlight mixes in with the mist in the trees,
bringing changes, bringing tears.

Together we have planted

In this first winter of our married life
we have planted hundreds of trees together;
we have set out in all weathers
carrying the hard paraphernalia:
spades and stakes, tubes and hammers;
and the softer gifts: small trees, love.

We have worked the land together,
selecting spots, digging holes, hammering stakes;
older trees, looming in the mist,
looked down in silence on our planting;
they have seen our minor disputes,
and the spreading effects of our husbandry.

In this first winter of our married life
we have returned home in all weathers,
much of the hard paraphernalia left behind;
we have exercised the softer gifts;
what will grow and not grow remains unknown,
but, together, we have planted with love.

I am a sieve

I am a sieve in the flow:
the shape and pattern of my holes
creates the turbulence that is my gift to this world.

The flow is endless:
there is no need to create,
creation is already infinitely here;
there is only opening to the flow that exists,
and shaping the turbulence that results.

I am a channel:
the qualities of the holes I make in myself
shape the beauty of my turbulence;
the particular weave of ripple.

The flow is me:
sometimes I pause a while mid-flow
and shape a part of me as a sieve;
a pattern in me makes more patterns:
what joy.

The troubled North Sea, 1942

Psalm 77
Verse 1   *I cried unto God with my voice, even unto*
                   God with my voice; and he gave ear unto
                   me.
Verse 16   *The waters saw thee, O God, the waters saw*
                   thee; they were afraid: the depths also were
                   troubled.
Verse 19   *Thy way is in the sea, and thy path in the*
                   great waters, and thy footsteps are not
                   known.

O Lord, thy sea is so troubled, so vast and dark;
protect we few as we cast ourselves upon thy sea tonight.

O Lord, look after our boat, Melampus (ML 1065);
keep our look-outs sharp, our engineer efficient,
our weaponry working;
and help our officer make the right decisions,
and not be too bold.

May the Germans not find us tonight before we find them,
for they will kill us if they can,
and we must try and kill them too.

May our engines continue to roar and throb
for the next twelve hours without cease,
making our heads ache.
O Lord, when we really need it, help us hit high speed fast,

keep our seventy foot launch driving through the waves,
twisting and turning,
making our bones vibrate with the hammering.

O Lord, please help our plywood hull keep out the waves,
even if it cannot keep out the German ordnance.
Help the enemy tracer miss our fuel tanks
so that we do not burn fiercely, lighting the night
until the dark waves quench us.

O God, help us return by morning
to this dreary east coast port that we love.

O Lord, spare me tonight, and the next nights;
I have a good woman to find and love and marry;
I have two sons who wait to be conceived.

We are a little afraid here, and troubled to our depths;
our way is in the sea, but we know not our footsteps;
O God, I cry unto Thee with my voice, even unto Thee with
my voice;
O God, give ear unto me.

The one who meditates is like a steward

The one who meditates is like
a steward at the entrance to the shrine room.

The steward stays at his post while people come in and out;
his job is to stay at the door and be present;
crowds may come in, and, later on, crowds may go out,
but he has to avoid joining them going in or out,
if he wants to remain at his post.

The one who meditates is like
a steward who is always leaving his post.

The people who come in and out of the shrine room
are very interesting, and include old friends;
the steward finds himself carried along in the crowd;
he may be sitting in the dining room enjoying lunch,
when he wakes up to his neglect, and hurries back.

The one who meditates is like
a steward who is privileged to watch over the shrine room.

At quiet times, when all the people have gone,
he can bask in the softness of emptiness;
in the silence he can hear the faint echoes of the teachings;
the benign wisdom of the ancestors suffuses the space;
in the quiet, that which is most precious is available to him.

The one who meditates is like
a steward who has found liberation at his post.

Lessons in wholeheartedness

When I was a young man, about twenty, not yet very
knowing,
I gave as much of my heart as I could to someone.
She, very beautiful to me, responded in kind,
but being slightly older, gave slightly less.
And so the affair played out over time.

In the confusion, pain, and relief of a long drawn-out ending,
it's not clear what happened to the heart I had given.
I think most of it I called back in,
but I left a part of it behind, perhaps deliberately,
because I had loved her so much.
And I think she did the same, though slightly less so.

As a young man, growing older, not yet very knowing,
I tended to think my heart was finite,
and that if a remnant had been left behind,
there was therefore less available for someone else.
And so I loved less than I might.

Now that I'm older, and a little less unknowing,
I have listened to the wisdom of my children,
who have given me an inkling of how my heart functions:
it seems that if I give my whole heart in the right way,
my heart grows bigger, not smaller.
I am willing to experiment, though old habits die hard.

We'll see how this affair plays out over time.

The one who breathes

You who would meditate
may like to befriend your breathing.

As though across a crowded room
you may see the one who breathes;
when you make your way to them,
the one who breathes smiles and offers help,
takes your hand and breathes with you.

The one who breathes
is alive even in the midst of suffering;
stands firm in the swirl of confusion,
offers love in the midst of anguish.

You who would meditate
will need a source of love;
across a crowded room
seek out the one who breathes;
the one who breathes is always here.

Little boy of nine

Little boy of nine, grieving for your father,
I know what faces you, but only my love reaches back
through the years;
I cannot tell you what you must discover for yourself.

He is dead, he is dead; it is a mystery that lasts for ever.
He never returns, and 'never' is the harshest word.
His warmth is gone, his voice is gone, his love is gone.

You will pray to God for his return,
and God is kind, and listens, but does not act.
Alone, you will search for the missing father you love
in the furthest darkness of the void, and find only emptiness.

You will wonder if he has secretly been taken away to be
cured,
and keep looking out for him on every street corner,
in case he reappears, but he does not
and instead his memory fades through the years.

Your sadness too will fade, but not die;
tears will continue to come upon you suddenly,
and their energy will rush through you, a flash flood of grief.
In the end, your capacity for sadness
will just be part of who you are,
neither looked for, nor resisted.

I am sorry to say this, but there will be little succour from others.
You will grow wise in the ways people shut off from death,
and you will become skilful at protecting them from their own discomfort;
but from those few who can look you in the eye,
and feel the depths of pain with you, and not flinch away,
you will learn the greatest love.

Alone, you will take a vow of life-long misery, from loyalty to the dead,
not knowing that he would want you to live life to the joyous full,
out of his love for you, and your love for him.
You will eventually unbury the vow and dissolve it,
but there will be lost joy.

Little boy of nine, there is much for you to find out of pain and grief,
and this life has given you an early start.
Only you can go inside and discover this reality that is yours.
It's a lot to ask, but it seems to be required.
I send you my love reaching back through the years,
I send you my love reaching back through the years.

So I never saw his body

So I never saw his body, waxy, white, and still;
and I never saw the coffin, heavy wooden box,
lifted carefully from the hearse by unknown men in black
suits;
and I never sat in the utilitarian crematorium chapel,
and heard the vicar grapple with the words and prayers,
and fail to do justice to my father's life;
and I never joined in with the thin voices of the few
mourners
attempting to sing the selected hymns;
and I didn't see the adult tears of grief,
and the dabbing of the eyes, and the struggles to constrain;
and I didn't stand around in the January cold afterwards,
wondering what to say, when there is nothing adequate to
say;
and I never saw the anonymous box of ashes,
final transformation of a life of vibrancy and love,
being scattered on the earth by path x, avenue y.

All this, being then considered too young, I was protected
from,
with the most loving of intentions;
instead there was created a black hole of unknowing
out of which emerged my own childish versions of unreality
which wormed their way into my life,
and from which nothing could protect me.

Here on Holy Island

Here on Holy Island the wonderful tide
cuts off the traffic for five hours twice every day:
no humming metal boxes driving in or out,
unusual peace and tranquillity emerging instead.

If only the tide could do a similar job on our thoughts,
cutting out the traffic for five hours twice a day,
allowing inner peace and tranquillity to manifest.
How might we not come closer to God?

Here on Holy Island the lives of the saints are all around
and the past brings its ruins into today.
St Cuthbert is gone, as are his warrior kings,
and the Vikings who craved for riches, not God.

The God of St Cuthbert is gone too,
along with the battles, the demons, and the killings.
Cuthbert's bones are relics now, curiosities;
our healing miracles now take place every minute in the
NHS.

You will not find his God here on Holy Island.
His God is not in the sea or waves or birds,
nor in the beauty of the seals singing.
His God is not in the warmly read words of the bible.

The past will deaden you if you let it.
In this moment when I know I am God,
and we know we are God,
and all knows it is God, then God is.

Our language is not old English, or biblical;
our monastery is global, our teachings wide-open to truth;
our God is not-two, not separate;
our Cuthberts are alive, and contemplating
in the fullness of all that is now known.

The wonderful tide on Holy Island turns again,
and again, and again.

I left the door ajar for God, and Death walked in

I left the door ajar for God, and Death walked in;
behind him I saw the shadowed forms
of those I might once have known.

In the silence that followed, I found myself explaining
how I always try to have him in mind;
how I sit when I can in the graveyard
with the dead bodies at rest all around;
that I keep with me the remains of those
who have gone before.

'I am making ready to join your crew,' I affirmed.
I looked Death in the eye, and he smiled kindly;
behind him I saw the shadowed form of God.

Leave the door ajar for Death, and God may enter.

She blooms, she blooms

Wake up each morning and create more beauty in the world:
start with her heart and pump it full of love,
admire her beauty, and bring poetry to her being;
she blooms, she blooms
who else will find her beautiful when you're gone?

Laugh into her eyes until they sparkle,
set her dancing so that she swirls through the day,
leaving her radiance lingering on all in her wake;
she blooms, she blooms
who else will find her beautiful when you're gone?

Hwaet! Listen to the spring!

Hwaet! Listen to the spring!
Hear the squabblings of the sparrows in the eaves, chirp-
chattering, pert-prating,
hear their fluttering in the guttering, new-nesting, mad-
mating;
hear the wildling warbling of the curlew, the long-beaked
one, woe-full,
calling to the ancestors, late-loved, long-lamented,
wandering the shore of shells;
hear the croak of the crows, clouded, crowded, dark-
shrouded creatures,
harsh-creaking with the carrion-lives of their raw-fleshed
ravagings.

Listen! Hear it all. Hear each one.
It comes, it's here, it's gone.

Like the faintest of breezes on the fine skin of your limbs,
it comes, it's here, it's gone.

Hear back, deep within each sound, the echo of Thor's
hammer, the big bang,
hear God's voice, singing to you, singing to you.
It comes, it's here, it's gone.

Too many sheds?

The shed was a thing of beauty when it came together,
manifesting from old wood out of three other sheds
including the donkey house in the field.
Those sheds were themselves made from older ancestor
sheds.
There was also an old window frame from the house,
and an old chicken shed door from a friend.
I hammered the nails in creatively,
and a shed of beauty shaped itself.

The shed was a thing of beauty when it de-shedded.
As I unbuilt it I admired the changes ten years had wrought:
here the work of penetrating wet under failed felt,
creating rotting wood fibre out of once-solid roof planks;
here the hundreds of holes of rampant wood worm,
gorging themselves, leaving dusty tunnelled weakness;
here the bright nails I hammered in, now pulled out,
magically become beautiful rust-brown accretions.

The empty space of potential is now the thing of beauty.
The re-usable wood stored, some rusty nails in a jar,
the window frame leaning against the oil tank: all waiting.
My human energy is currently engaged elsewhere,
but plans are slowly bubbling under,
and the shed-building tradition is deep-rooted.
The next beautiful shed-coming is sure to happen.
I have an idea for a privy.

Coughing meditation

Sit up in bed on a grey morning.
Be with your breathing.
Focus your attention on a particular spot
at the back of your throat, and wait.

Notice when the smallest of tickles
manifests there – from nothing –
and starts to grow rapidly into a bigger tickle.

Observe in wonder how your coughing reflex takes over,
how in a moment you are hacking and spluttering,
your body wracking itself in convulsive movements.

You are catapulted into a different state of mind.
If you are fortunate, phlegm is catapulted into your mouth,
and may be spat out on to a piece of bog roll.

Your body is still, peace returns.
Sit quietly with your breathing
focussing on the back of your throat, waiting.

Love, work, and knowledge

To love on a honeymoon is easy.
But the crucial time to love is much later,
when the other one looks ugly,
and is pissed off with you,
and you're exhausted by the wrestling.
To love then is life-changing,
to love then builds up your power to love.

You can become a super-lover
by working out against the resistance
by manifesting love through their resistance, and yours.

To work whole-heartedly on a new project is easy:
you can be carried along by the wave of excitement.
But the crucial time to work whole-heartedly
is when work has lost its point,
and your work-mates have become gossipy cynics,
and you spend your time planning to get away.

In the work-gym of high resistance,
your heart can become more and more whole,
and the world can start to transform.

The prophet said, 'work is love made visible'.
Maybe he also said,
'love is very hard work, made subtle.'

Hey, hey, PJA, how many enemies did you make today?

Who is thine enemy?
If thou makest any into thine enemy,
canst thou not make all into thine enemies:
if not now, then in the days to come?

If thou makest any into thine enemy
(and all may be made into thine enemies)
is not the whole world against thee,
and art thou not sorely troubled?

Would'st thou live without enemies?

Then find thine enemies within,
and make of them friends.
They wait only on love
which, thou knowest, is easily given.

A father's prayer

And ah my beautiful children,
how much I love you,
and how deeply grateful I am
to have had this chance to be your father,
and to have loved you as I do.

And when I go, likely before you,
in one thing let us be sharply clear.

While, from time to time
you may mourn, and be sad,
it is my dearest wish, my guidance,
my prayer, and my will and testament,
that you continue
to make joy, and generate love,
and laugh, and play, and sing,
as we have oftentimes done together.

Do this for yourselves, and others,
or, if you like, do this in remembrance of me,
that I may look on and say:
I am their father, these are my children,
they love life and all within it,
and in this, in them,
I am well pleased.

The bramble tangle

You need a certain amount of aggression to take on a
bramble tangle.
I fought a good fight with one down by the river;
it was taking over the path, threatening, scratchy.
My weapons were secateurs and a sickle,
my defence was thick leather gloves.
I approached warily, poking away from a distance.
We are bramble, we are the strength of tangle;
we prickle, we grow, we prickle, we die back.
Snip, snip; I'm cutting; snip, snip; I'm cutting,
and pulling out great lengths, and carefully putting them
aside;
snip, snip, I'm in there, chopping wherever I can reach;
I'm scratched, blood to bramble, bramble gets me.

The way is growing clearer as I take the thicket apart.

I'm admiring how cleverly the bramble tangle works:
last year's dark green stems rest on top of the dark brown
stems
from the year before; the dark brown stems are supported
on the light brown stems from the year before that;
each layer spread on a lower layer to grow higher, and
further.

We are not separate individuals sprung purely from the earth;
we spring from layers of bones that support us,
we sprawl across the skeletons of those who have grown before.

Our ancestors grew on and died back
and then some more came and grew on.

We prickle, we grow, we prickle, we fruit, we die back.

A massive tangle of thought-structures fruited into secateurs,
and with those in hand, I fought a few rounds.

At the end, exhausted, we were tangled up in an embrace,
our blood and sweat mixed together.
Now I could not love the bramble tangle more.

Good Friday 2011, looking northwards from my window

Easter is late this year though the ash is still bare
while on the hawthorns the leaves are bright.
Gragareth looms faintly through the haze in the distance
awaiting revelation from the morning light.

I could take my ease on the grassy bank in the early sun.
Later the stones poking through would slowly appear
and later still the ants that come to bite and eat.
Peace and suffering intertwine around here.

The three telegraph poles with their long trailing wires
form three odd crosses though no-one's hung on there to
bleed;
but there's no denying that God and Jesus
sit deep in my being if not in my creed.

I could ride from here in any direction
as though I understood the sacrifice of the Son.
But there's years of practice still to do:
in truth I'm very far from done.

Splitting for the world

I remember when those few of us split from Africa across
the Red Sea.
We stayed on the beach, eating shellfish and stuff,
till we got too many, then another bunch of us split off,
and we headed for the next beach, fresh and new.
Eventually we beachcombed our way to the rest of the
world.

I remember when I was little, splitting from my mum and
family
to try out the next beach at primary school.
I made a home with friends there till the time came to move
on again,
we split up and went on to secondary schools:
new worlds, different beaches.

I remember many splits in my life, and each new group
was the right place to be, till the time came to go.
I remember trying to stay in touch, but the coastal trek
was too long, and the distances too great.

Now I find I am required to recognise
that my home is not a beach but this pattern:
I move in, I love and laugh, I learn and fish, I move on;
I move in, I sit and pray, I listen and speak, I move on;
I move in, I am, I am different, I have already moved on.

Every year I rise again from the dead

On Easter Sunday a figure appeared in my inner world.
He took me aside and showed me
how often I acclaim myself in triumph there,
manifesting as the special one.

We looked at the times also that I betray myself,
selling my integrity for a sum that can never be enough.

Again and again in the garden of my mind,
I attack my enemies, who turn out to be myself in the end,
so that I have to work hard to heal the self-inflicted wounds.

I saw how every year I try to kill off my capacity for life
in order to fit in with what the authorities in me require,
and I saw how my mother mourned the loss,
because, having loved me so much,
she knew the potential I was sacrificing.

I have scorned myself, and scarred myself,
and clumsily tried to stop everything, out of misplaced pity.

At critical points, I was not there for my son,
as my father was not there for me, and I cried.

Leaving myself for dead,
I have laid myself to rest in a cave,
and blocked out the world.

But every year I roll away the stone,
every year I rise again from the dead,
every year life renews itself within me,
and will not be denied, despite my best doubts.

In the end the figure turned to me and said,
'Unless we know we are God,
God cannot know he is us'.

What was revealed

On a sunny Easter Sunday this was the revelation.
In the stone lobby of the meeting house, in the gloom,
behind the notice frame taken down in order to replace the
notice,
was a bat, clinging to the wall,
small, furry, brown, upside down as the books say,
wings folded, tiny feet attached to the rough of the stone,
twitching a little in the light, waiting for twilight,
and the liberation of flight.

On a sunny Easter Sunday this was the revelation.
In the peace of the meeting room,
behind the silence and the sitting,
was the presence of God, strange, unknown,
waiting to be revealed, as the books say,
through sound from the silence,
light from the shade,
and loosening from the clinging to this life,
that may lead to unlikely liberation.

The commitment of the lark

And as I walked down the slopes of Ingleborough
in the early freshness of an April morning
the larks rose in front of me, one by one,
and sang their way upwards against the blue of the sky.

I stood and watched, and listened,
and rose with them, above my terrain,
leading my life in the fullness of wing and beak,
displaying all that I have, the strength of my feathers,
then, song ended, sinking back down to the moor.

If I commit to the path before me I find freedom.
If I back away from the difficulties
I gain the illusory freedom of the fugitive,
skulking, evading capture, leading a lesser life.

The lark launches into air, wind, and song.
May I manifest the commitment of the lark.

A short biography

My family heritage is the north of England, but I was born in the early '50s in Portsmouth, where my dad was based (he was in the navy; see *The troubled North Sea, 1942*).

He had a serious accident when my brother and I were little, and he was in Stoke Mandeville hospital for 15 months (*Lessons from Aylesbury*). He came home to live with us again after we moved to Leeds, and died when I was nine (*Little boy of nine; So I never saw his body*).

My mother had an extensive and supportive family and I was fortunate to spend time with many of my relatives, particularly at Tranmire, near Whitby, where I loved to spend holidays (*Snared by tradition; How to hold back, how to let go; And what happened to you little boy?*).

Later we moved to Cheshire, and I went to school in Sandbach, where I discovered I was good at English, but really preferred rugby.

I studied English at a very traditional university, an interesting experience for someone unfamiliar with that kind of environment.

I failed to follow a conventional career, and instead tried to pursue what Buddhists, I later learned, call 'the career of understanding'.

Since then I've lived in London, Birmingham, Lifespan, Sheffield, and, for the last 25 years, Bentham, near Lancaster.

I've earned my living in community work, therapy, the voluntary sector, and public health. And other bits and pieces.

One of my delights has been, as a father, to help introduce three new beings to this world (*Cupped hands; As, on a starry Christmas night; We fathers; The freedom in keeping still*).

Over the years inspirational guides, particularly Thich Nhat Hanh, Ken Wilber, and Arnie Mindell, have kept me sane and kept me challenged.

My poetry is one of the territories within which I try to come to terms with the challenges they and other teachers set me. Sometimes this is a playful process, sometimes a wrestling match. Always it is about doing the recommended practices, utilising the maps, exploring, noticing what happens, and learning.

I have valued the following approach: try things for yourself, and find out for yourself, but value the wisdom of those who have gone before.

While I have dabbled in poetry occasionally over the years, these poems all came in the year following my marriage to Mary Swale, my partner of 25 years. So thanks in particular to my beloved wife for her creative inspiration.

Lightning Source UK Ltd.
Milton Keynes UK
UKOW052041220312

189431UK00002B/2/P